Cultural Traditions in

Iran

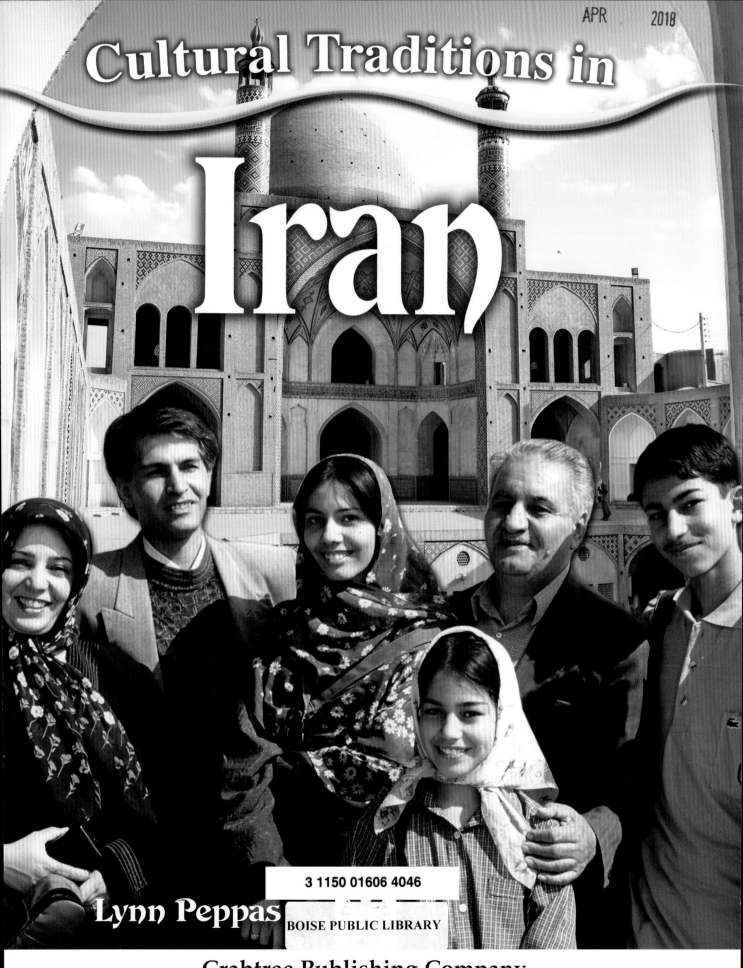

Lynn Peppas

Crabtree Publishing Company

www.crabtreebooks.com

Crabtree Publishing Company

www.crabtreebooks.com

Author: Lynn Peppas
Publishing plan research and development:
 Reagan Miller
Editor: Kathy Middleton
Proofreader and indexer: Wendy Scavuzzo
Photo research: Tammy McGarr
Production coordinator and prepress technician:
 Tammy McGarr
Print coordinator: Margaret Amy Salter

Cover: Interior of Imam Mosque ceiling (top); Iranian sweets, zoolbia, bamieh, and dry fruits (bottom middle); Kebab dish (bottom left); The Sultan Salahuddin Abdul Aziz Shah Mosque, also known as Blue Mosque (background); Imperial fritillary flower (middle right); Ney Turkish reed flute sufi (middle far right); A decorated oboe style instrument (right); Iranian dancers (top left and right); Iranian drum called a dhol (bottom right); Young girls in traditional clothes (middle)

Title page: Agha Bozorg school and mosque in Kashan, Iran (background); an Iranian family (front)

Photographs:
AP Images: Vahid Salemi: p8; Kamran Jebreili: p10
Bridgeman Images: ©World Religions Photo Library p7
Corbis Images: ©Yves Gellie: p6; ©ABEDIN TAHERKENAREH/epa: p11; ©Ahmad Halabisaz/Xinhua Press: p20; ©Morteza Nikoubazl/ZUMA Press: p21; ©Morteza Nikoubazl/Reuters: p24;
Getty: BEHROUZ MEHRI: pp12, 13, 18; ATTA KENARE: pp15, 19, 23; Anadolu Agency: pp26, 27
iStock: Cover (bottom right), (top left and right)
Keystone: ZUMAPRESS.com/ ©Morteza Nikoubazl: p22;
Shutterstock: ©JPRichard: cover (top); ©Artography: p4; ©Neftali: p15 (middle left); ©Zurijeta: p17; ©Lefteris Papaulakis: p29; ©Asianet-Pakistan: p30; Cover (background), Title page (background), pp4 (map), 19 (bottom right), 20 (bottom right), 24 (bottom right), 28
Superstock: Kaehler, Wolfgang: title page; Kristian Cabanis / age footstock: p5; Credit: Marka: p14;
Thinkstock: Charlotte-Amelie: Cover (middle left); p16, p25 (top right)
Wikimedia Commons: Safoura_Zoroofchi: p9; Bahraam Roshan: p25; Public Domain/www.bbcpersian.com: p29 (bottom right); Public Domain/ Jami al-Tawarikh: p31

Library and Archives Canada Cataloguing in Publication

Peppas, Lynn, author
 Cultural traditions in Iran / Lynn Peppas.

(Cultural traditions in my world)
Includes index.
Issued in print and electronic formats.
ISBN 978-0-7787-8061-8 (bound).--ISBN 978-0-7787-8066-3 (pbk.).--ISBN 978-1-4271-9959-1 (pdf).--ISBN 978-1-4271-9954-6 (html)

 1. Holidays--Iran--Juvenile literature. 2. Iran--Social life and customs--Juvenile literature. 3. Muslims--Social life and customs--Juvenile literature. I. Title. II. Series: Cultural traditions in my world

GT4874.A2P46 2015   j394.26955   C2014-907787-4
                                            C2014-907788-2

Library of Congress Cataloging-in-Publication Data

Peppas, Lynn.
 Cultural traditions in Iran / Lynn Peppas.
 pages cm. -- (Cultural traditions in my world)
 Includes index.
 ISBN 978-0-7787-8061-8 (reinforced library binding : alk. paper) --
 ISBN 978-0-7787-8066-3 (pbk. : alk. paper) --
 ISBN 978-1-4271-9959-1 (pdf) --
 ISBN 978-1-4271-9954-6 (html)
 1. Festivals--Iran--Juvenile literature. 2. Holidays--Iran--Juvenile literature. 3. Iran--Social life and customs--Juvenile literature. I. Title.

 GT4874.A2.P46 2015
 394.26955--dc23
                                            2014046722

Crabtree Publishing Company

www.crabtreebooks.com   1-800-387-7650

Printed in Canada/042015/EF20150224

Published in Canada
Crabtree Publishing
616 Welland Ave.
St. Catharines, ON
L2M 5V6

Published in the United States
Crabtree Publishing
PMB 59051
350 Fifth Avenue, 59th Floor
New York, New York 10118

Published in the United Kingdom
Crabtree Publishing
Maritime House
Basin Road North, Hove
BN41 1WR

Published in Australia
Crabtree Publishing
3 Charles Street
Coburg North
VIC 3058

Contents

Welcome to Iran

Iran is a country on the continent of Asia. It is located in a region called the Middle East. More than 60 million Iranians live there. Iran used to be called Persia. Most Iranians speak Persian and practice a religion called **Islam**. People who follow Islam are called Muslims. Most Muslims in Iran are Shia Muslims. A smaller group, called Sunni Muslims, lives there, too.

Muslims worship Allah, which is the Muslim name for God. They worship in buildings called mosques, like this one in Isfahan, Iran.

Starting at age nine, Muslim women are expected to cover their heads with a scarf called a hijab. In Iran, they also wear loose coats over pants. At home, some women wear clothes similar to those worn by North American women.

Iran is an **Islamic state**. This means that the country's laws follow Islam's holy book called the Quran. Most holidays in Iran usually celebrate the life or death of Muslim religious leaders. Some Iranians follow other religions such as Judaism, Christianity, or Zoroastrianism. While Iranians share many **traditions**, each religious group has its own unique traditions.

Did You Know?
The dates of religious holidays in Iran are figured out using the Islamic calendar, which has fewer days than the international calendar. This means some holidays fall on different days from year to year.

Family Celebrations

Today, most men and women can decide who they want to marry. Couples who live in cities often choose Western-style clothes for their wedding. Wedding dinner parties sometimes last for more than one day. Young people who can't afford big weddings sometimes say their vows with hundreds of other couples in a government ceremony.

Did You Know?
It is a custom in Iran to grind sugar onto a scarf over the couple's head, and for the bride and groom to feed each other a spoonful of honey to bring sweetness to their marriage.

It is a tradition that the first words a new baby should hear is the Muslim call to prayer. The call to prayer is a command to stop and pray that is called out from mosques five times every day.

Women's Day and Mother's Day

Wives and mothers have a special day held on the birthday of Fatima, the daughter of Islam's **prophet** Muhammad. Husbands thank their wives, and children show appreciation to their mothers. Women receive flowers, gifts, or handmade crafts.

Nowruz (New Year)

Nowruz, which means "new day," is the New Year holiday in Iran. Persian New Year is celebrated on March 20 or 21—the first day of spring. Giving to others during Nowruz is a tradition meant to bring good luck in the New Year. Children often receive gifts. Families enjoy eating traditional dishes such as *fesenjoon*—a walnut and pomegranate stew. The pomegranate is a fruit grown in Iran since ancient times.

Chaharshanbe Suri, or Wednesday Feast, is part of the New Year celebration. Also known as the Festival of Fire, it includes such customs as jumping over a bonfire or flying paper lanterns filled with hot air while making a wish for the year to come.

Haft Seen tables, such as the one shown here, are set to look as beautiful as possible.

Haft Seen is the ancient custom of setting a Nowruz table in Iran. It is decorated with seven things that begin, in Persian, with the letter "s." Items on a Nowruz table include a mirror, apples, candles, water, vinegar, garlic, goldfish, coins, and the Quran.

Did You Know?
Growing wheat or lentils in a dish during Nowruz is a tradition called *sabzeh*. It is a symbol of new growth in the New Year.

Islamic Republic Day

Islamic **Republic** Day, also called National Day, is a holiday that celebrates the founding in Iran of a government ruled by the laws of Islam. On April 1, 1979, Iranians were asked to vote on whether they wanted to live by rules according to the religion of Islam. Almost all Iranians voted yes, and a new **constitution** was written for the country.

Iranian women are shown here voting.

Women carry Iranian flags on Islamic Republic Day in the capital city of Tehran.

Islamic Republic Day is held each year on April 1 or March 31. Iranians celebrate their country by watching parades and fireworks, going on picnics, and gathering in public squares to listen to speeches.

Did You Know?
Iranians celebrate Islamic Republic Day as the turning point of their nation's independence and freedom.

Sizdah Bedar

Sizdah Bedar, or 13 Bedar, falls 13 days after Nowruz or New Year. In Iran, it is also known as Nature Day because it is a time for families to go outside and enjoy nature. People head for parks and wooded areas to play games such as soccer and backgammon. *Sizdah Bedar* means "getting rid of 13." The custom on this "13th" day is to get rid of bad luck.

On this holiday, many families enjoy picnics in parks or in areas near streams.

Sports and games are fun ways to spend time outdoors on 13 Bedar.

The sabzeh (see page 9) is thrown away on Sizdah Bedar, in a stream if possible. This tradition rids the home of any sickness or bad luck collected during the first twelve days of the New Year. No one else should touch or take another person's sabzeh, or they might take on that family's bad luck.

Did You Know?
Girls often tie knots out of grass and make a wish about their future husbands. Young married couples do the same to wish for a baby.

Holidays Honoring Ayatollah Khomeini

Ayatollah Khomeini was an imam, or Muslim leader, in Iran. He was Iran's first leader after the country became an Islamic Republic in 1979. Iranians celebrate this holiday, called the Magnificent Victory of the Islamic **Revolution** of Iran, every year on February 11. On that day, many Iranians go to see movies, concerts, or art and museum shows about Ayatollah Khomeini.

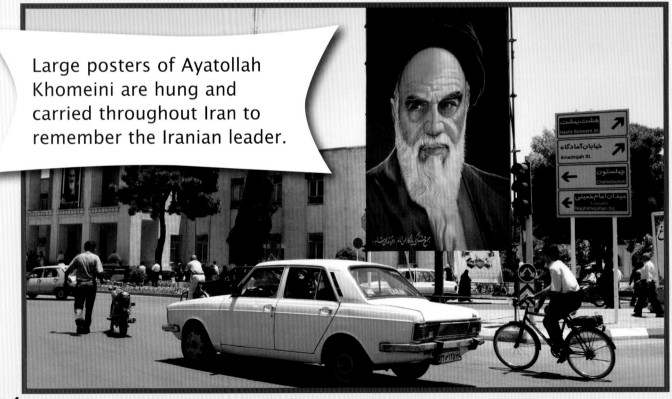

Large posters of Ayatollah Khomeini are hung and carried throughout Iran to remember the Iranian leader.

Ayatollah Khomeini is featured on Iran's money and postage stamps.

Since his death in 1989, Iranians have remembered Ayatollah Khomeini on June 4 each year. Many wear black clothing and wave black flags to show their sadness at his passing.

Eid al-Adha

Eid al-Adha, also called Eid-e-Ghorban in Iran, is a religious festival that occurs about 70 days after Ramadan. The festival celebrates the **sacrifice** made by the Islamic prophet Ibrahim to prove his faith to Allah. On Eid al-Adha, special prayers are said and a goat or sheep is **slaughtered** as a sacrifice. Families have a feast and give some of the meat away too.

Biryani is a popular dish eaten on Eid al-Adha. It is made with lamb and rice.

Muslims travel to Mecca to perform religious duties. One duty is to walk seven times around this building called the Kaaba. Muslims believe it was built by Ibrahim and his son.

Eid al-Adha also marks the end of Hajj, which is a five-day period when many Muslims visit the holy city of Mecca in Saudi Arabia. Every Muslim is expected to go on a **pilgrimage**, or journey, to Mecca at least once in their lifetime.

Did You Know?
Muslims believe Allah asked Ibrahim to kill his own son as a sacrifice to prove his faith. When Ibrahim agreed to do as he was asked, Allah spared his son and allowed Ibrahim to sacrifice a ram instead.

Ramadan

Ramadan is the most important religious festival for all Muslims. It lasts one month and falls on different dates every year according to the Islamic calendar. Ramadan is a time when people try to **purify**, or clean, their thoughts and actions. One way Muslims do this is by **fasting** for most of the day. Fasting allows people to know what it is like to be hungry so they will be more generous to less fortunate people.

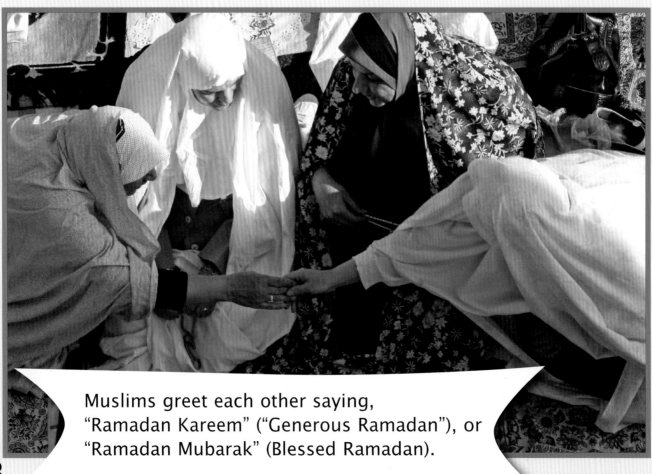

Muslims greet each other saying, "Ramadan Kareem" ("Generous Ramadan"), or "Ramadan Mubarak" (Blessed Ramadan).

This Iranian family is enjoying their *Iftar*, or evening meal. Children are not expected to fast, but they usually try to.

During Ramadan, people eat an early breakfast called suhoor. Breakfast foods include bread, eggs, cheese, tea, and dates. Then, all Muslims are expected to fast during daylight hours from sunrise to sunset. After the sun has set, they eat a meal called iftar, which is usually a thick Iranian soup or stew called *ash*.

Did You Know?
In Iran, Muslims do not expect non-Muslims to fast during Ramadan. But they do expect others to not eat or drink in front of them!

There is no public holiday for Ramadan in Iran, but many businesses open for fewer hours than usual. Streets and shops are decorated with lights and flowers. Iranian people like to say "the guest is God's friend." People invite family, friends, and neighbors to visit, and they give food to others. Guests are sometimes treated to a Persian dessert called *sholeh zard*, which is a saffron rice pudding. Children like to eat traditional sweet pastries such as *zoolbia* and *bamieh* (see below) at Ramadan.

These families are eating after sunset at Ramadan in the square of a mosque.

Reading the Quran is an important activity especially during the last ten days of Ramadan. That is when Laylat al-Qadr takes place. Muslims celebrate it as the day when the prophet Muhammad received Allah's words from an angel. These words are the first writings of the Quran.

Praying regularly and reading the Quran is very important during Ramadan. Some Muslims read the entire Quran at this time.

Did You Know?
Laylat al-Qadr means "Night of Power." Muslims believe that on this night Allah and the angels protect, forgive, and grant the prayers of Muslims.

Eid al-Fitr

Eid al-Fitr is a two-day holiday for Iranians. It is a happy celebration for Muslims that marks the end of Ramadan, or "breaking of the fast." It falls on the day after Ramadan ends. Many Muslims get up early to go to a special religious service at a mosque. Sometimes a service is held in a large open field. This gives thousands of people enough room to gather together for prayers and to celebrate the end of Ramadan.

Thousands of people say Eid al-Fitr prayers together in the city of Tehran.

This girl shows off her new outfit at Eid al-Fitr prayers.

Muslims greet one another and say "Eid Mubarak," which means "Blessed Eid." It is a tradition on this day to wear new clothes to prayer. There are also rules that must be followed according to the Islamic religion. Fasting is not allowed on Eid al-Fitr. In addition to attending prayer together, Muslims are also required to give food or money to the poor.

Cultural Festivals

Some festivals in Iran celebrate the changing of the seasons and have been celebrated for thousands of years! The Festival of Yalda, also called Shab-e Chelleh, is celebrated on the first night of winter, around December 21. Some Iranians stay up all night with family and friends playing games, eating fruits, and reading poems by the Persian poet Hafez. This festival honors the birth of the ancient sun god Mithra.

Around October 1, most Iranians celebrate the harvest festival Mehregan. It is a day to give thanks for the food collected for the cold winter months ahead. This man is offering nuts to the Mehregan guests.

Iranians celebrate Tirgan with singing, dancing, and poetry readings. Swimming and splashing in water is a fun way for people to enjoy the Rain Festival.

Tirgan, or the Rain Festival, is held around July 2 or 3. *Tir* means "arrow." This midsummer festival is associated with the legend of a disagreement over the border between Persia and another country. The two countries chose an **archer** to shoot an arrow, then drew the border where it fell. Afterward, it began to rain on the **drought-stricken** lands.

Ashura

Ashura is a religious holiday. It falls on a different day each year and is a national holiday in Iran. For Shia Muslims, Ashura is a solemn day to remember the death of the Muslim leader named Imam Hussein, the grandson of the prophet Muhammad. He died during a historic battle at Karbala over 1,000 years ago.

Some Muslims remember Hussein's death by placing black banners and flags on buildings and streets in Iran.

Iranians gather and show signs of sadness as they walk through the streets.

Did You Know?
For Sunni Muslims, Ashura marks the day when Muhammad declared that Muslims should fast. Sunnis fast on this day.

Because Ashura is a day to remember suffering, no entertainment or weddings are allowed to take place. Shia Muslims walk through the streets wearing black. Some take part in a **passion play** about the battle of Karbala. Forty days later, another holiday called Arbaeen is held honoring Hussein's death.

27

Oil Nationalization Day

Oil **Nationalization** Day is a public holiday in Iran. Nationalization is when a government takes control or ownership of something for the benefit of the country. Oil is Iran's main **natural resource**. On March 20, Iranians celebrate the day Iran's government took control over the country's oil **industry**. The holiday is sometimes called Petroleum Day. *Petroleum* is another word for oil.

Oil is used to make fuel for vehicles and airplanes, as well as many other products.

This postage stamp from the 1970s shows gas pipelines being built across Iran.

Before it was nationalized, other countries or companies were making money from Iran's oil industry. Iran received only a little of that money. A law was passed in Iran on March 20, 1951, that allowed the country's government to control all of its oil industry. Many Iranians feel this was an important event in their country's **independence**.

In 1951, Iran's Prime Minister Mosaddeq led the movement to nationalize Iran's oil industry.

Birthday of Muhammad

Muhammad is a prophet of Islam. Shia and Sunni Muslims celebrate Muhammad's birthday on different dates within the same week. Instead of celebrating on just one day, former leader, the Ayatollah Khomeini, made the holiday in Iran into **Unity** Week to unite, or bring together, all Muslims in the country.

Both Sunni and Shia Muslims put aside their differences with one another during Unity Week.

Laylat al-Isra wa al-Miraj is another religious holiday in Iran based on Muhammad. It is tradition on wa al-Miraj to tell someone the story of Muhammad's journey from Mecca to Jerusalem, and his visit to the seven heavens before returning to Mecca on that day.

Unity Week begins on the day Sunni Muslims believe Muhammad was born. It ends on the day that Shia Muslims believe that Muhammad was born. During this time, some Muslims gather together to read the Quran. They go to mosques to attend special services that praise Muhammad.

Did You Know?
Unity Week, which started in Iran, is celebrated by many Muslim communities throughout the world today!

Glossary

archer Someone skilled using a bow and arrow

constitution Laws of a nation

drought-stricken Without rain for a longperiod of time

fasting To not eat food; often for religious reasons

independence Not ruled by another country

industry A group of companies that produce the same kind of product

Islam A religion practiced by Muslims that follows one God through the teachings of the prophet Muhammad

Islamic state A country in which the laws follow the holy book of the religion of Islam

nationalization When a government takes control or ownership of something on behalf of the country

natural resource A material found in the earth

passion play A dramatic recreation of suffering or death

pilgrimage A long walk or journey to a holy place

prophet A person who brings Allah's words to many people

republic A type of government that gives its people the power to decide how their country is run

revolution A sudden or complete change in government

sacrifice To offer something precious to Allah, such as the life of an animal

slaughter To kill an animal

tradition The beliefs or customs that are held by a group of people

unity Being joined together

Index